Table of Contents

Introduction..
Ihram..3
Physical Purity..3
Ihram Garments..3
Miqat..4
Salah al-Ihram...4
Niyyah..4
Talbiyah..5
Violation & Penalties...5
Haram of Makkah..5
Entering Makkah...6
Entering Masjid al-Haram..6
First Sight of the Kaaba..7
Tawaf al-Umrah...8
Preparation...8
Starting Point..8
Intention...9
Start the Tawaf..10
Raml...10
Dhikr & Dua..10
End of Circuit at the Hajar al-Aswad..11
During Tawaf...11
Complete the Tawaf..11
Salah...11
Zamzam...12
Multazam...13
Sa'i...13
Proceed to Safa..14
Make Dua at Safa...14
Proceed to Marwa...15
Dhikr & Dua..15
Make Dua at Marwa..16
End of Sa'i...16
Dua and Salah..16
Leave the Haram...16
Halq or Taqsir...16
Remember to take with you...18
List of things for Hajj & Umrah..19
Virtues of Madinah..20
The etiquette of Madinah...20
Don't Miss out in Madinah...21
Ziyarats..22
Places in Makkah to Visit...22
Places in Madinah to Visit..23

Introduction

All praise is due to Allah, and peace and blessings upon His messenger Muhammad (صَلَّى ٱللَّهُ عَلَيْهِ وَسَلَّم).

This brief but comprehensive pocket guide is presented to you to outline the rituals of Umrah. It contains all the necessary information regarding the methods, rights and formalities of Umrah.

Umrah consists of four essential practices. Firstly, you get changed into the Ihram garments before the Miqat, perform two Rakahs of Salah and make your Niyyah as the Miqat approaches, thereafter reciting the Talbiyah frequently. Secondly, you perform Tawaf al-Umrah of the Kaaba followed by two Rakahs of Salah, preferably near Maqam Ibrahim. Thirdly, you do Sa'i of Safa and Marwah. Lastly, you shave (Halq) or shorten (Taqsir) your hair, allowing you to leave the state of Ihram and complete your Umrah.

Ihram

Please refer to this article to learn more about the Ihram and its prohibitions.

Physical Purity

Before getting changed into the Ihram garments, take care of your personal hygiene by clipping your nails and removing the hair under your armpits and beneath the navel. You should then do Ghusl, a highly emphasised Sunnah for those intending to enter into a state of Ihram. If you can't perform Ghusl, doing Wudhu will suffice. Men may apply Attar/perfume to their heads/beards, ensuring not to get any on the Ihram garments. This should all be carried out at your place of residence before your flight (assuming you're flying).

Ihram Garments

You will then get changed into your Ihram garments which for men consist of two, normally white, clean seamless pieces of cloth. The sheet which wraps around the waist covering the lower body is known as the Izar, and the sheet that is draped over the upper body like a shawl is known as the Rida. Sandals shouldn't cover the heel and ankle. The Hanafi school of thought stipulates that the top part of the foot should also remain exposed.

Ensure you put on your Ihram attire before crossing the designated Miqat. You will likely be travelling to Saudi Arabia via plane, so it is advisable to get changed into your Ihram at the airport prior to departure or during a stopover if you have one. Check in first and get changed in the prayer room or bathroom. Alternatively, you can put on your Ihram in-flight although bear in mind that aeroplane bathrooms are usually very limited in space, and there may well be a rush of people intending to do the same thing as the Miqat approaches. If you decide to change into your Ihram attire on the plane, do so at least an hour before the Miqat is crossed.

Miqat

You may delay making your intention until the Miqat approaches. Just before crossing, remove any articles of clothing that you may still be wearing that violate the conditions of Ihram, such as socks, headwear and underwear.

Women aren't required to conform to a specific dress code. Clothing should be normal modest Islamic dress with a head covering of any colour. Hands and faces must remain exposed, although socks may be worn.

Note: if you're going to Madinah before Makkah, you don't need to enter into the state of Ihram at this point. You will do so after your stay in Madinah.

Salah al-Ihram

It's Sunnah to perform two Rakahs of Salah before entering into the state of Ihram. This can be performed after getting changed at the airport or in-flight before crossing the Miqat, providing there are prayer facilities on-board. Observe the prayer with the intention of performing two Rakahs Nafl for Ihram.

Since you're not yet in the spiritual state of Ihram, the prayer may be observed with the head covered. It is recommended to recite Surah al-Kafirun (Surah 109) in the first Rakah and Surah al-Ikhlas (Surah 112) in the second, although other Surahs may be read. Don't forget to make Dua after this Salah.

Niyyah

The Niyyah for Umrah should be made at the Miqat or close to it as you move in its direction. Ideally, you should delay making the intention until the last moment so you aren't restricted by its prohibitions for longer than need be. It is recommended (Mustahabb) that you make the intention verbally, as well as reiterating it internally.

Following are three examples of intentions that may be uttered in Arabic:

لَبَّيْكَ اللَّهُمَّ عُمْرَةً

Labbayka llāhumma 'umratan.
O Allah, here I am to perform Umrah.

اللَّهُمَّ إِنِّي أُرِيْدُ الْعُمْرَةَ

Allāhumma innī urīdu l-'umrata.
O Allah, I intend to perform Umrah.

اللَّهُمَّ إِنِّي أُرِيْدُ الْعُمْرَةَ فَيَسِّرْهَا لِي وَتَقَبَّلْهَا مِنِّي

Allāhumma innī urīdu l-'umrata fa yassirhā lī wa taqabbalhā minnī.
O Allah, I intend to perform Umrah, so accept it from me and make it easy for me.

Talbiyah

After making your Niyyah, you must recite the Talbiyah to validate your intention and enter into the state of Ihram. The utterance of the Talbiyah is Wajib according to the Hanafi and Maliki schools of thought. The Shafi'i and Hanbali schools consider it a Sunnah.

You must recite the Talbiyah at least once after making your intention for Umrah. Failure to do so will result in an invalid Umrah!

The Sunnah method of reciting the Talbiyah is to briefly pause at four places, indicated by the dashes. The prayer is as follows:

– لَبَّيْكَ اللَّهُمَّ لَبَّيْكَ –لَبَّيْكَ لَا شَرِيكَ لَكَ لَبَّيْكَ – إِنَّ الْحَمْدَ وَالنِّعْمَةَ لَكَ وَالْمُلْكَ – لَا شَرِيكَ لَكَ

Labbayka llāhumma labbayk(a), labbayka lā sharīka laka labbayk(a), inna l-ḥamda wa n-ni'mata, laka wa l-mulk(a), lā sharīka lak.

At Your service, Allah, at Your service. At Your service, You have no partner, at Your service. Truly all praise, favour and sovereignty are Yours. You have no partner.

Talbiyah

After uttering the Talbiyah, you will now be in the state of Ihram and be known as a Muhrim. Make sure you're well aware of the prohibitions of Ihram and ensure you don't fall foul of its rules. If a rule of Ihram is violated, Damm or Sadaqah will be required as expiation.

Violation & Penalties

It is recommended to send Salawat on the Prophet صَلَّى ٱللَّٰهُ عَلَيْهِ وَسَلَّمَ after reciting the Talbiyah and to make Dua for yourself and others. Continue reciting the Talbiyah for the rest of your journey until you reach one of the doors Masjid al-Haram prior to performing Tawaf.

Haram of Makkah

The Haram of Makkah is a sacred area that extends a number of miles around Masjid al-Haram in all directions. In this area, it is forbidden to:

- •Cut or damage grass, trees or any other type of vegetation.
- •Harm or kill wild animals. This includes scaring away pigeons and other birds.
- •Carry weapons.
- •Fight or behave in a way that will violate the sanctity of this area.

Although you're unlikely to breach one of these rules, keep in mind the sanctity of Makkah.

Note: If you intend to perform an additional Umrah later on, you must assume Ihram outside the boundary of the Haram before going back to Masjid al-Haram to perform Umrah. Many choose to enter into Ihram at Masjid Aisha, which is the nearest and most convenient location from Masjid al-Haram. Transportation to get there is available near the mosque.

Entering Makkah

As you reach the limits of the Haram, constantly recite the Talbiyah, do Dhikr and send Salawat upon the Prophet صَلَّى ٱللَّهُ عَلَيْهِ وَسَلَّمَ. Recital of the following Dua is recommended upon entering the Haram:

اَللّٰهُمَّ هَذَا حَرَمُكَ وَأَمْنُكَ فَحَرِّمْنِي عَلَى النَّارِ، وَأَمِنِّي مِنْ عَذَابِكَ يَوْمَ تَبْعَثُ عِبَادَكَ وَاجْعَلْنِي مِنْ أَوْلِيَائِكَ وَأَهْلِ طَاعَتِكَ.

Allāhumma hādhā ḥaramuka wa amnuka fa ḥarrimnī ʻala-n-Nār, wa amminnī min ʻadhābika yawma tab'athu ʻibādak, wa jʻalnī min awliyā'ika wa ahli ṭā'atik.
O Allah, this is Your sanctuary and security, so make me unlawful to Hell-Fire, make me safe from Your punishment on the day You resurrect Your servants, and make me one of Your friends and one of the people who obey You.
After arriving at your accommodation in Makkah, you may want to freshen up or take a rest before making your way to Masjid al-Haram to perform Tawaf al-Umrah. If you decide to take a shower, ensure you don't use any items that are prohibited in the state of Ihram, e.g. scented soap or shampoo. It is recommended you present yourself at Masjid al-Haram as soon as possible.
When you're ready, decide which of your belongings you want to take with you, bearing in mind there are thieves that operate in the mosque.
Tip: It is recommended that you take a drawstring bag for your shoes. Keep them close to you because they can get lost fairly easily.

Entering Masjid al-Haram

It is Sunnah to enter Masjid al-Haram via Bab al-Salam (the Gate of Peace). This may not be possible as the authorities have designated entrances to the mosque for pilgrims performing Umrah. If you can't do this, you may proceed through any other door. Step through with your right foot first and recite the supplication for entering a mosque. Either or both of these supplications may be recited:

بِسْمِ اللهِ، اللَّهُمَّ صَلِّ عَلَى مُحَمَّدٍ. اللَّهُمَّ اغْفِرْ لِي وَافْتَحْ لِي أَبْوَابَ رَحْمَتِكَ.

Bismi-llāh, Allāhumma ṣalli alā Muhammad. Allāhumma-ghfir lī wa-ftaḥ lī abwāba raḥmatik.
In the name of Allah, send prayers upon Muhammad صَلَّى ٱللَّهُ عَلَيْهِ وَسَلَّمَ. O Allah, forgive me and open for me the doors of Your Mercy.

أَعُوذُ بِاللهِ الْعَظِيمِ، وَبِوَجْهِهِ الْكَرِيمِ، وَسُلْطَانِهِ الْقَدِيمِ، مِنَ الشَّيْطَانِ الرَّجِيمِ

Aʻūdhu bi-llāhi-l-Aẓīm, wa bi-wajhihi-l-karīm, wa sulṭānihi-l-qadīm, mina-sh-Shayṭāni-r-rajīm.
I seek protection in Allah the Tremendous, His Noble Countenance, and His pre-eternal Sovereign Might from Shaytan the rejected.
Notes:

- Don't perform Tahiyatul Masjid (prayer for greeting the mosque) if you intend to; your Tawaf will suffice as the "greeting" for Masjid al-Haram.
- If you don't have the intention of performing Tawaf immediately, you may perform Tahiyatul Masjid.
- In Masjid al-Haram, it is permissible for anyone to walk across those performing Salah. However, their place of prostration should be avoided.

First Sight of the Kaaba

After entering the mosque, keep your gaze lowered until you reach the Mataf area, which is the open space where Tawaf takes place. When you're ready, with humility, awe and reverence, lift your gaze to set sight on the beatific vision of the Holy Kaaba.

Upon seeing the Kaaba for the first time, raise your hands and make Dua with the utmost concentration and sincerity, as this is among those places where prayers are answered. Remember to recite Salawat upon the Prophet صَلَّى ٱللَّهُ عَلَيْهِ وَسَلَّمَ when making Dua. Umar ibn al-Khattab I narrated:

Dua is suspended between heaven and earth and none of it is taken up until you send blessings upon your Prophet صَلَّى ٱللَّهُ عَلَيْهِ وَسَلَّمَ.

[Narrated in Sunan al-Tirmidhi]

Imam Abu Hanifa I would use this opportunity to make Dua to Allah that he be among those whose supplications are always accepted.

Recite the following three times:

اللهُ أَكْبَرُ. اللهُ أَكْبَرُ. لَآ إِلَهَ إِلَّا اللهُ.

Allāhu akbar. Allāhu akbar. Lā ilāha illa-llāh.

Allah is the Greatest. Allah is the Greatest. There is no God except Allah.

It's a Sunnah to recite the following Duas:

اَللَّهُمَّ زِدْ هَذَا الْبَيْتَ تَشْرِيفاً وَتَعْظِيماً وَتَكْرِيماً وَمَهَابَةً، وَزِدْ مَنْ شَرَّفَهُ وَكَرَّمَهُ مِمَّنْ حَجَّهُ أَوْ اعْتَمَرَهُ تَشْرِيفاً وَتَكْرِيماً وَتَعْظِيماً وَبِرّاً.

Allāhumma zid hādhā-l-Bayta tashrīfan wa ta'ẓīman wa takrīman wa mahābah, wa zid man sharrafahu wa karramahu mimman ḥajjahu awi-'tamarahu tashrīfan wa takrīman wa ta'ẓīman wa birrā.

Allah, increase this House in honour, esteem, respect and reverence. And increase those who honour and respect it—of those who perform Hajj or 'Umrah—in honour, respect, esteem and piety.

اَللَّهُمَّ أَنْتَ السَّلَامُ وَمِنْكَ السَّلَامُ، حَيِّنَا رَبَّنَا بِالسَّلَامِ.

Allāhumma Anta-s-Salāmu wa minka-s-salām, ḥayyinā Rabbanā bi-s-salām.

O Allah, You are Peace and from You is peace. Make us live, Lord, in peace.

Do Dhikr, make Dua and send Salawat upon the Prophet صَلَّى ٱللَّهُ عَلَيْهِ وَسَلَّمَ in abundance here. Make the most of this opportunity before you begin your Tawaf, especially if it's the first time you've set eyes on the Kaaba.

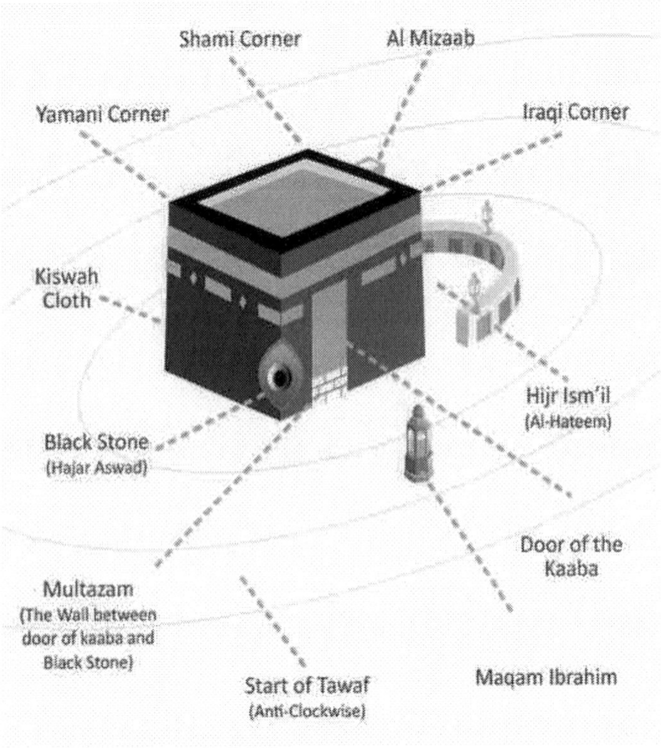

Tawaf al-Umrah

For the Tawaf to be considered valid, the following is necessary:

1. To perform Tawaf yourself.
2. To make an intention (verbally or not).
3. To do Tawaf in Masjid al-Haram.
4. To be in a state of Wudhu and free of anything that requires Ghusl, e.g. menstruation.
5. To conceal the Awrah.
6. To start Tawaf from Hajar al-Aswad.
7. To move in an anti-clockwise direction.
8. To avoid the Hatim (the semi-circle area outside the Kaaba).
9. To perform Tawaf by foot, for those who are able.
10. To perform seven circuits.
11. To perform two Rakahs of Salah after the Tawaf.

Preparation

Ensure you're in a state of Wudhu, and if you're a male, uncover your right shoulder by passing the top sheet of your Ihram under your right armpit, allowing the garment to hang over your left shoulder (Idtiba).

Starting Point

Position yourself in line with the corner of the Kaaba where the Hajar al-Aswad is situated. This corner is the one that faces a single minaret (the other three corners face two minarets). There is a green light on the wall of the Masjid opposite the Kaaba, which indicates where the Tawaf starts from. This is the starting point of each Shawt (circuit). Stand just before this starting point facing the Kaaba.

Intention

As with any other act of worship, make the Niyyah to perform Tawaf solely for Allah. You may also ask for acceptance and ease of your Tawaf. The following words may be said:
O Allah, I intend to perform the Tawaf of Umrah of the Kaaba for your sake and your sake alone. Please accept it from me and make it easy for me.
You may make the following intention, which is in Arabic:

اللَّهُمَّ إِنِّي أُرِيدُ طَوَافَ بَيْتِكَ الْحَرَامِ فَيَسِّرْهُ لِي وَتَقَبَّلْهُ مِنِّي

Allāhumma innī urīdu l-ṭawwafa baytika l-ḥarāmi fa yassirhu lī wa taqabbalhu minnī.
O Allah, I intend to perform Tawaf of your Sacred House, so make it easy for me and accept it from me.
The Niyyah doesn't have to be verbal.
Kissing, Touching or Saluting the Hajar al-Aswad (Istilam)
Although kissing the Hajar al-Aswad is very virtuous, don't harm others around you in an attempt to reach it.

•**Kissing** – If you reach the Hajar al-Aswad, place your hands on it, put your face between your hands, say "bismi llāhi wallāhu akbar (بِسْمِ اللَّهِ وَاللَّهُ أَكْبَرُ)" and kiss it lightly. Some scholars have said it is preferable to kiss it three times if you have the chance.

•**Touching** – If you're in reaching distance but unable to kiss it, touch it with your hand(s) and kiss your hand(s).

•**Saluting** – If it isn't possible to reach the stone, as is likely to be the case, perform a symbolic Istilam from afar by directly facing the Hajar al-Aswad and raising your hands up to your earlobes (as you would do when starting Salah). Ensure your palms are also facing it, as though your face and hands are on the Hajar al-Aswad, and say "bismi llāhi wallāhu akbar (بِسْمِ اللَّهِ وَاللَّهُ أَكْبَرُ)." You may kiss your palms if you wish.

If you decide to attempt to kiss or touch the Hajar al-Aswad, it is important to be aware that the experience can be quite intense. Due to the large number of people gathered around it, there is often a significant amount of pushing and shoving, which can potentially lead to injuries. It is nearly impossible to reach the Hajar al-Aswad without having to force your way through people vying to reach the sacred stone.

The following supplication, a Dua of Ali I, may be recited when coming parallel to the Hajar al-Aswad in each circuit:

بِسْمِ اللَّهِ وَاللَّهُ أَكْبَرُ، اللَّهُمَّ إِيمَاناً بِكَ وَتَصْدِيقاً بِكِتَابِكَ، وَوَفَاءً بِعَهْدِكَ وَاتِّبَاعاً لِسُنَّةِ نَبِيِّكَ مُحَمَّدٍ

Bismi llāhi wa llāhu akbar, Allāhumma īmānan bika wa taṣdīqan bi kitābika wa wafā'an bi ahdika wattibā'an li sunnati nabiyyika Muḥammadin صَلَّى ٱللَّهُ عَلَيْهِ وَسَلَّمَ.

In the name of Allah, Allah is the greatest. O Allah, out of faith in You, conviction in Your book, in fulfillment of Your covenant and in emulation of Your Prophet's Sunnah صَلَّى ٱللَّهُ عَلَيْهِ وَسَلَّمَ.

Other forms of Dhikr, such as Tahlil (lā ilāha illā Allāh) and Salawat upon the Prophet صَلَّى ٱللَّهُ عَلَيْهِ وَسَلَّمَ may also be uttered at this point.

Start the Tawaf

Turn to your right and start the first circuit of your Tawaf, ensuring the Kaaba is on your left. Proceed in an anti-clockwise direction and avoid walking through the Hijr Ismail. If you happen to walk through it, the circuit won't count, and it will have to be repeated.

Raml

In the first three circuits, men should perform Raml, which is the practice of walking briskly, lifting the legs forcefully and sticking out the chest. However, if there is congestion, which is likely to be the case if you're closer to the Kaaba, only perform this Sunnah if you're sure you won't harm or inconvenience others. During peak times, you're unlikely to be able to perform this action.

Dhikr & Dua

During your Tawaf, you may recite prayers and supplications of your choice. Duas are accepted during Tawaf, so make the most of the occasion and remember Allah with sincerity and devotion. It's perhaps advisable not to read from a Dua book, especially if you don't understand the Arabic. Imam Ibn Hibban said:

Specifying a Dua would take the moment away, because with specific Duas, one will merely be repeating words, whereas this occasion is for any Dua and for remembering one's Lord with humility and sincerity.

Thus you should supplicate in any language and in any manner that you prefer. If you want to make Quranic and Prophetic supplications during your Tawaf, make an effort to memorise and learn the meanings of them. Reciting Quran and sending Salawat upon the Prophet صَلَّى ٱللَّهُ عَلَيْهِ وَسَلَّمَ during Tawaf is also recommended.

Upon reaching the Rukun-al-Yamani (the Yemeni Corner), the corner preceding the Hajar al-Aswad, touch it with your right hand or both hands and say “Allāhu akbar (اللّٰهُ أَكْبَرُ)” if you manage to get close enough. If there’s too much congestion, as is likely to be the case, proceed without saying Takbir or gesturing towards it.

It is a Sunnah to recite the following Dua between the Rukn al-Yamani and the Hajar al-Aswad:

رَبَّنَا آتِنَا فِي الدُّنْيَا حَسَنَةً وَفِي الْآخِرَةِ حَسَنَةً وَقِنَا عَذَابَ النَّارِ

Rabbanā ātinā fi d-dunyā ḥasanatan wafi l-ākhirati ḥasanatan wa qinā ‘adhāba n-nār.
O our Lord, grant us the good of this world, the good of the Hereafter, and save us from the punishment of the fire.
[Surah Al-Baqarah, 2:201]

Imam Shafi’i recommended this Dua to be recited throughout the Tawaf.

End of Circuit at the Hajar al-Aswad

Returning to Hajar al-Aswad marks the completion of one circuit. Begin the second by doing Istilam of Hajar al-Aswad as previously described and saying “Allāhu akbar (اللّٰهُ أَكْبَرُ)”. You should say Allāhu akbar while doing Istilam in all subsequent circuits. You will be performing Istilam eight times in total during the Tawaf, one before the start of the Tawaf and one at the end of each of the seven circuits.

During Tawaf

The Tawaf should be completed in a continuous manner with no interruptions between circuits. However, if a congregational prayer is due to start, you must join the congregation and resume your Tawaf from the position that you stopped. The circuit need not be repeated. These rules also apply if you need to repeat your Wudhu.

Complete the Tawaf

Proceed in the same manner until you have completed seven circuits. Performing Istilam at the start of Tawaf and at the end is a highly emphasized Sunnah, and performing Istilam on the other six occasions is desirable.
If you are in a state of Idtiba, cover your shoulder with your Ihram.

Salah

Upon finishing the Tawaf, perform two Rakahs of Salah, preferably in a position where Maqam Ibrahim is between you and the Kaaba. However, keep in mind that since Maqam Ibrahim is situated within the Mataf, there is often nowhere for pilgrims performing Tawaf to move except around and almost over the top of those praying just beyond Maqam Ibrahim, resulting in a great

deal of congestion. If it isn't possible to perform the prayer there as a result of crowding, it can be performed anywhere in Masjid-al-Haram.
While moving to the place where you intend to perform the two Rakahs, it is recommended to audibly recite the following:

وَاتَّخِذُوا مِنْ مَقَامِ إِبْرَاهِيمَ مُصَلًّى

Wattakhidhu min maqāmi Ibrāhīma muṣalla.
And take the Maqam Ibrahim as a place of Salah.
[Surah al-Baqarah, 2:125]

It is Sunnah to recite Surah al-Kafirun (Surah 109) in the first Rakah and Surah al-Ikhlas (Surah 112) in the second, after Sura-al-Fatiha. Make sure you make plenty of Dua after completing the prayer.

Zamzam

After completing Salah and making Dua, drink your fill of Zamzam water which is available around the Tawaf area and from various water fountains and dispensers in Masjid-al-Haram. The entrance to the old well of Zamzam has been covered to allow for more room to do Tawaf.
The Prophet صَلَّى ٱللَّهُ عَلَيْهِ وَسَلَّمَ said: "The water of Zamzam is for whatever purpose it is drunk for." Before drinking the Zamzam water, make an intention that its consumption will be a means of fulfilling your wishes, whether that is good health, success in this world, or protection from the tribulations of the grave. When drinking the water, it is Mustahabb to stand and face the Kaaba, say Bismillah, pause to take a breath three times, and say Alhamdulillah after finishing. You can also rub it on your face and body. You may recite the following Dua after drinking the water:

اللَّهُمَّ إِنِّي أَسْأَلُكَ عِلْمًا نَافِعًا وَرِزْقًا وَاسِعًا وَعَمَلًا مُتَقَبَّلًا وَشِفَاءً مِنْ كُلِّ دَاءٍ

Allahumma innī as'aluka 'ilman nāfi'an, wa rizqan wāsi'an, wa 'amalan mutaqabbalan, wa shifā'an min kulli dā'.

O Allah, I ask You for knowledge that is beneficial, provision that is abundant and a cure for every illness.

You may also make any other supplication of your choosing as it's another station where Duas are accepted.

Multaltazam

After you have finished drinking Zamzam water, you may proceed to theMultazam, which is the area betweenHajar al-Aswad and the door of the Kaaba.
The Multazam is almost impossible to get to during Hajj season due to the large crowds that gather. However, it is sometimes accessible during other parts of the year.
If it is possible to reach the Multazam, raise your hands above your head, cling to the wall and press your chest and cheeks against it. It is a Sunnah of the Prophet صَلَّى ٱللَّهُ عَلَيْهِ وَسَلَّمَ and yet another station where supplications are accepted, so you should lengthen your Dua here.
If you can't reach the Multazam due to the crowds, you may face it and supplicate from a distance.

Sa'i

It is a Sunnah to perform Sa'i immediately after Tawaf, although you may take a break if you need to. If you feel tired after Tawaf or your feet are aching, you may take a rest until you feel you're ready. Remember, you will be covering over three kilometres during Sa'i, so make sure you have sufficient energy to complete the rite before starting.
For the Sa'i to be considered valid, the following is necessary:

1. To perform Sa'i yourself.
2. To have entered into Ihram before performing the Sa'i.
3. To stay in Ihram until the Sa'i has been completed.
4. To perform Sa'i at its correct time.
5. To begin Sa'i at Safa and finish at Marwa.
6. To perform Sa'i after having done Tawaf.
7. To perform Sa'i on foot unless you have a valid excuse.
8. To perform seven laps.
9. To cover the complete distance between Safa and Marwa.

Istilam of the Hajar al-Aswad
Before Sa'i, it is Sunnah to do Istilam of Hajar al-Aswad one last time. This will be the ninth time, following the eight times you performed Istilam during Tawaf.

If you’ve forgotten to perform this Istilam, or you’re finding it difficult to return to the line of the Hajar al-Aswad due to crowding or tiredness, it may be omitted. However, you can do Istilam anywhere else in Masjid al-Haram, as long as you’re facing the Hajar al-Aswad.

Proceed to Safa

Proceed to the hill of Safa, which is located inside Masjid al-Haram in line with the Hajar al-Aswad. There are signs which indicate where it is. As you’re approaching Safa, it is Sunnah to recite the following:

إِنَّ الصَّفَا وَالْمَرْوَةَ مِن شَعَائِرِ اللَّهِ

Inna ṣ-ṣafā wa l-marwata min sha’ā’iri llāh(i).

Indeed, Safa and Marwa are from the Signs of Allah. [Surah al-Baqarah, 2:158]

Then say:

أَبْدَأُ بِمَا بَدَأَ اللهُ بِهِ

Abda’u bimā bad’allahu bihi.

I begin with that which Allah has begun with.

These should only be recited once before Sa’i and not at the start of each lap.

Make Dua at Safa

Upon reaching the hill of Safa, face the direction of the Kaaba and raise your hands in supplication. Your view of the Kaaba may be obscured, so make an educated guess about its location and face this direction. Don’t raise your hands up to your earlobes or gesture towards the Kaaba as you would have done during Tawaf. You may say Takbir (Allāhu akbar), Tahlil (lā ilāha illā Allāh) and send Salawat upon the Prophet صَلَّى ٱللَّهُ عَلَيْهِ وَسَلَّمَ.

It is Sunnah to recite the following Dua:

اَللّٰهُ أَكْبَرُ، اَللّٰهُ أَكْبَرُ، اَللّٰهُ أَكْبَرُ، وَلِلّٰهِ الْحَمْدُ

Allāhu akbar, Allāhu akbar, Allāhu akbar, wa lillāhi l-ḥamd.

Allah is the greatest; Allah is the greatest; Allah is the greatest, and to Allah belongs all praise.

لاَ إِلَهَ إِلاَّ اللَّهُ وَحْدَهُ لاَ شَرِيكَ لَهُ، لَهُ الْمُلْكُ وَلَهُ الْحَمْدُ يُحْيِي وَيُمِيتُ، وَهُوَ عَلَى كُلِّ شَيْءٍ قَدِيرٌ

Lā ilāha illallāh waḥdahu lā sharīka lah(u), lahu l-mulku wa lahu l-ḥamdu yuḥyī wa yumīt(u), wa huwa 'alā kulli shay'in qadīr.
There is no deity except Allah, alone without a partner. To Him belongs the Dominion, and to Him belongs all praise. He gives life and death, and He has power over everything.

لَا إِلَهَ إِلَّا اَللَّهُ وَحْدَهُ، أَنْجَزَ وَعْدَهُ وَنَصَرَ عَبْدَهُ وَهَزَمَ اَلْأَحْزَابَ وَحْدَهُ

Lā ilāha illallāhu waḥdah(u), anjaza wa'dahu wa naṣara 'abdahu wa hazama l-aḥzāba waḥdah.
There is no deity except Allah alone. He fulfilled His promise, supported His slave and defeated the Confederates alone.
After reciting this Dua, you may recite your own supplications. Read the Dua a total of three times, making your own supplications in between each time, as was the Sunnah of the Prophet صَلَّى آللَّهُ عَلَيْهِ وَسَلَّمَ.

Proceed to Marwa

From Safa, make your way towards Marwa. Between Safa and Marwa, you will encounter two sets of green fluorescent lights approximately 50 metres apart, which indicate the distance that Hajar ran in order to get to higher ground. These two markers are known as Milayn al-Akhdharayn (the two green mileposts). Between these two lights, it is Sunnah for men to run at a medium pace while women should continue normally.

Dhikr & Dua

There is no fixed Dhikr or Dua that has been prescribed to be read during Sa'i, so you may recite any prayers or supplications of your choice and send Salawat upon the Prophet صَلَّى آللَّهُ عَلَيْهِ وَسَلَّمَ.

Make Dua at Marwa

Upon reaching the hill of Marwa, face the direction of the Kaaba, raise your hands in supplication and repeat the same supplications you recited at Safa.
This completes one lap of Sa’i. Returning back to Safa is considered a second lap.

End of Sa’i

Repeat this procedure until you have completed seven laps, at which point you should be at the hill of Marwa.

Dua and Salah

It is recommended to make a final Dua here and also to perform two Rakahs of Nafl Salah in Masjid al-Haram following Sa’i.

Leave the Haram

As you leave Masjid al-Haram, step out with your left foot and recite the following Dua, as was the Sunnah of the Prophet صَلَّى ٱللَّٰهُ عَلَيْهِ وَسَلَّمَ when leaving the mosque:

بِسْمِ اللهِ وَالصَّلَاةُ وَالسَّلَامُ عَلَى رَسُولِ اللهِ، اللَّهُمَّ إِنِّي أَسْأَلُكَ مِنْ فَضْلِكَ

Bismi llāhi, wa ṣ-ṣalātu wa s-salāmu ‘ala rasūli llāh. Allāhumma innī as’aluka min faḍlik.
In the name of Allah, and peace and blessings be upon the Messenger of Allah. O Allah, I ask of you from Your bounty.

Halq or Taqsir

After Sa’i, you must have your hair shaved (Halq) or trimmed by at least an inch (Taqsir) in order to leave the state of Ihram and complete your Umrah. It is more virtuous for a man to have his head shaved completely.

Women may only have their hair trimmed.

There are a number of licensed barbershops in Makkah, which are open 24 hours a day and generally only close during Salah times. There are many barbershops in the Zamzam Towers, Hilton shopping

complex and al-Safwa Towers. You will also see many barbers located outside the Marwah door after you finish Sa'i.
Alternatively, you may shave or trim your own hair in order to come out of the state of Ihram.

Congratulations on your Umrah!

You are now free from the restrictions of Ihram, and you may change into regular clothing. If you plan on performing another Umrah, you must travel to the boundary of the Haram in order to once again enter into Ihram. Most pilgrims choose to enter into Ihram at Masjid Aisha, which is the nearest and most convenient location from Masjid al-Haram. Taxis are available near the mosque.

Remember to take with you

NECESSARY	TOILETRIES	MEDICINES	MISC
Passport ticket and visa photocopies	Miswak, Toothbrush, toothpaste	Regular medication	Universal Adaptor
Vaccination card	Non-perfumed Soap, shampoo	Tablet for nausea, vertigo	Alarm clock/phone
Money	Brush, comb	Pain relief	Earplugs
Important contact numbers	Nail cutter, scissors	Throat lozenges, anti-allergy	Eye mask
Small Quran and Dua book	Pocket tissues, wet wipes (unscented)	Cold &Flu relief	Small mirror
Mobile phone and charger	Deodorant	Antibiotic	Snacks, biscuits etc
	Vaseline, lotion	Band-Aids	Zip lock bags
Sleeping bag or chattai	Sanitizer	Anti-bacterial cream	
	Safety pins		

List of things for Hajj & Umrah

- Start walking before UMRAH
- Light Color Bhurqas
- Light Color Scarfs (for ladies)
- Comfotable cloths even these are western but not objectionable
- No high voltage utensils
- Wash cloth by onself because laudry is expensive
- Leather socks
- Cross bag for documents
- Soft back pack
- Document photocopy in every lugage and original is safe separate place
- Quran & islamic Books at decent place
- Scissor & Safelty rasor
- nail cutter
- Electric extension
- shampoo, soap, hand wash, tooth brush, tooth paste etc
- needle & thread
- safety pins
- Tawaf tasbeeh
- Electric kettle
- tea bags + tea whitner
- rusk, biscuits & snacks
- Disposible utensils and disposible dasterkhawan
- one plate
- one cutlery
- medicine according to health issue
- pain killers, panadol, cough and sneezing medicine
- Sun block
- better to decide meetup point it will help if at any point if somebody got lost
- better to be in sabar in whole journey
- Always be alert in all cases. dont ever trust blindly

Virtues of Madinah

Many pilgrims do not understand the importance of Madinah. Nor do they value the time spent there. Every believer should have the love of Madinah in his heart. He should hope and pray to meet his end in the beloved city of the Prophet (صَلَّى آللّٰهُ عَلَيْهِ وَسَلَّمَ).

The Prophet (صَلَّى آللّٰهُ عَلَيْهِ وَسَلَّمَ) and his Companions loved Makkah and hated to leave it. But Allah planted the love of Madinah in their hearts.

After the Conquest of Makkah, RasoolAllah (صَلَّى آللّٰهُ عَلَيْهِ وَسَلَّمَ) chose to return to Madinah and made it his final home. He would pray to Allah to bestow blessings on this sacred city.

Madinah is a sanctuary. Its trees should not be cut and no innovations should be introduced here, nor any sins committed. Whoever does so will incur the curse of Allah, the angels and all the people.

Madinah is also referred to as Madinah al-Munawwara (City of Light), Madinat-un-Nabi (City of the Prophet) (صَلَّى آللّٰهُ عَلَيْهِ وَسَلَّمَ) and Taiba (pure, pleasant). The old name of the city was Yathrib.

One Salaah in the Masjid-un-Nabi is equal to a thousand salaahs in any other masjid. The Messenger of Allah (صَلَّى آللّٰهُ عَلَيْهِ وَسَلَّمَ) had such immense love for Madinah that whenever he was returning from a journey, he would make his horse go faster as soon as he would draw close to the holy city.

Beneath the sacred soil of Madinah lies the blessed body of the final Messenger (صَلَّى آللّٰهُ عَلَيْهِ وَسَلَّمَ) and the remains of thousands of his Companions. Whoever has the means to die in Madinah should do so, for the Prophet (صَلَّى آللّٰهُ عَلَيْهِ وَسَلَّمَ) shall intercede on behalf of everyone who dies here or is buried in Jannat-ul-Baqi.

The etiquette of Madinah

- To visit Madinah with the right intention, not as a casual tourist.
- To be involved in righteous deeds like recitation of the Quran, Zikr, Dua, Durood, Sadaqah, pursuit of sacred knowledge, Dawah , assisting others and other such activities.
- To keep oneself away from sin and vain activites.
- To remain in a state of purity (wudhu), and to smell pleasant, and to wear decent attire.
- To send durood on the Prophet (صَلَّى آللّٰهُ عَلَيْهِ وَسَلَّمَ) abundantly.
- To be in a state of humility and submission to the Rabb.
- To be in a state of gratitude for having the opportunity of being in the blessed city.
- To display the best of manners.
- To speak in a low tone within the Masjid-e-Nabvi.

- To be careful not to waste food, water, etc. Even water, a precious commodity, should be used sparingly for wudhu and bathing.
- To be careful not to litter in the sacred city. A misdeed becomes magnified in this holy place.
- To make sure we don"t step over people or jump over them in order to secure a place in the Masjid.
- To ensure we don"t pray in walkways or pathways.

Don’t Miss out in Madinah

- Every time you enter the Masjid, pray two units called Tahiyattul-Masjid (unless the time is Makruh).
- Visit the grave of the blessed Prophet (صَلَّى ٱللَّهُ عَلَيْهِ وَسَلَّمَ) and offer salaam to him and his two Companions.
- Visit Masjid-e-Quba and pray nafil salaat there. 2 units of prayer here earn the reward of one Umrah.
- Visit the martyrs of Uhud. Pray for them and offer salutations to them.
- Visit Riyadh-ul-Jannah (piece of Jannah) situated next to the grave of the Prophet (صَلَّى ٱللَّهُ عَلَيْهِ وَسَلَّمَ). Pray two units here. Do not push, shove, or exhibit rough behavior.
- Visit Jannatul-Baqi which is the graveyard outside the Masjid-e-Nabvi. Here lie buried the remains of the Prophet„s family and thousands of His Companions. Pray for their forgiveness and ask Allah to elevate their ranks. Make dua that we should also join them and be raised with them on the Day of Judgment

Ziyarats

Places in Makkah to Visit

- Masjid e Aisha
- Jannat al Mualla
- The Cave of Hira
- Jabl Nur in Makkah
- Cave of Thaur
- Zubaida Canal
- Masjid Jinn
- Bilal bin Rabah Mosque
- Mount Abu Qubais
- Masjid Al Khayf
- Jabal Rahma
- Masjid Al Nimra
- Muzdalifah
- Jamarat
- Grave of Sayyidah Maymuna
- Masjid Al Hudaibiyah
- Al-Shabeka Graveyard
- Tuwa well
- The Kiswa Factory
- Clock Tower Museum
- Makkah Museum
- Exhibition of the Two Holy Mosques Architecture
- Masjid al Bay’ah

Places in Madinah to Visit

- Masjid al Nabawi
- Jannat ul Baqi
- House of Fatima bint Hussain
- Uhud Mountain
- Mount of archers جبل الرماة
- Uhud Mountain Cave
- Mount Thawr جبل ثور
- Masjid Ghamama
- Quba Walkway
- Masjid Quba
- Masjid Al Dirar
- Ethq Well بئر عذق
- Masjid Musabbih
- Masjid Qiblatain
- The Seven Mosques
- Cave of Bani Haram
- Dar Al-Madinah Museum
- Wadi e Jinn
- Uthman bin Affan well
- Hejaz Railway Museum
- Fort Kaab bin Ashraf
- King Fahd Quran Printing Complex
- Beer e Shifa
- Masjid Bani Haram
- Castle of Urwah bin Zubair
- Mount Ayr جبل عير

- Salman Al Farsi Garden
- Ghars Well
- Alyasira Well
- Saeed bin Al Aas castle
- Khyber Fort
- Badr Battleground

for more details visit **https://www.faysalkhan.org**

Printed in Great Britain
by Amazon

46989087R10015